The Only Mindset Book You'll Ever Need for Network Marketing Success

It's NOT your Attitude – It's your Mindset!

David Williams

The Only Mindset Book You'll Ever Need for Network Marketing Success

Copyright © 2014 by David Williams

ISBN 978-1500666972

Table of Contents

What is the biggest problem faced by networkers today?

It's a lack of production. Forget anything else you have been worrying about – leads, closing, lacking the will to follow-up, being effective on the phone, etc, etc; at the end of the day it's all about production.

All problems in networking can be solved by an increase in production.

That is what we are going to solve.

And in case you're wondering - production is any action you need to do to achieve income success in your company.

Guess what? In networking, a lack of production is really just a behavioral problem.

It is not an attitudinal problem.

Behavior is something we do.

Attitude is something we feel.

Now the term 'behavioral problem' may sound like something an adolescent experiences and parents endure, but each of us face challenges in our behavior during our entire life. But as far as we networkers are concerned the lack of production is strictly behavioral. It's all about how we behave.

And this is what we will learn to master through Mindset.

Why do we feel unable to pick up the phone, answer an email, or follow-up with a prospect?

Long before we decided to join our network marketing company we were accustomed to our normal, everyday life – good or bad. We were accustomed to things that we were familiar with - like our family, our evenings free, sleeping in on the weekends, and yes, worrying about bills...

Hey, each of us is genetically coded to like things the way they are. We don't like change, we actually like things to be 'the same'. We are all programmed this way.

Many people even brag, "Oh, I don't like change."

Look, it's genetic, don't feel bad – it's in our DNA.

In the distant past, change usually led to a bad outcome. And those who changed too much often ended up dead. Those who stuck to one thing that worked for them usually did OKAY.

But in the last 100 years, the world has changed far quicker than in the previous 4,000.

It's very hard to change when our DNA is whispering in our ear 'stay the same'.

We have been taught by our upline that 'for things to change, we have to change'. This is so simplistic that it's almost false since nobody teaches you *how to change*.

There is a much simpler and easier way to increase production than 'changing your attitude and expecting different results', and I'll show it to you.

What is the Lotto Ticket Attitude to Wealth?

I want you to remember back, back to the time you were looking for an opportunity. When you first considered joining a networking company.

I want to you to imagine how you felt about your life. You might describe your situation as 'not making enough money' - we are all familiar with that. Each of us is or was familiar with that feeling of not having enough money. We had the 'lack of enough money' feeling so entrenched that it seemed normal to us. It was 'normal' to go without or to live on borrowed money. And being normal brings contentment. It's sad but it's a fact.

You see, any change will require some discomfort. Big change will bring 'big discomfort'.

None of us want discomfort. We are not willingly go and do anything that will cause us discomfort.

Now we still desire more money but we really don't want to have to change anything in our life to get it. We just 'desire' change.

So by desiring more money - but by doing nothing - we end up with zero additional cash. So what happens? We do something that takes little effort - with no change - to get us what we desire...

For example we go out and buy a lottery ticket.

That's not change.

It's easy because it causes little discomfort: just the price of a ticket.

We need to understand that real long term money only comes with real change.

The Five Hidden Aspects of Change – and attitude isn't even one of them!

1) For us to get more money we need to change.

2) Change brings discomfort.

3) We resist anything that causes discomfort – even if it's something we desire

4) Results without change are fleeting.

5) We need to change our behavior which means accepting discomfort to get what we desire (and not depend on motivational seminars for the fleeting boost of attitude they bring - they are only a 'pick me up'.)

We must now determine what we must do to replace – change – old behavior.

And determining that new behavior is the subject of our next chapter.

my objective

What is the ULTIMATE objective of sponsoring some-one? (Most people never get this)

other people's time, resource
Network energy

What is our objective as networkers?

Now, I'm not asking 'what is our task' – what is our objective as a networker?

Real network marketing is truly about one objective only: effectively tapping into other people's networks, time, energy and resources. That's what we do. Your sponsor sponsored you with the idea that you could prospect your circle of influence with your program. _cold mkt: time + resources_

NOTE: If you sponsor someone who tells you they are only interested in working the cold market, you are tapping into their time and resources, (money to create leads). Not everyone wants to tap into their warm market – but even so there is a lot they can bring something to our business. A long time ago I got over 'forcing' the warm market approach. _cold mkt – tap into ideas, resources_

That is really what it's all about. If you are prospecting in the cold market – you desire to sponsor someone who had some contacts that you and she/he can effectively tap into. If they have no warm market we can into their knowledge, into their ideas, and into their resources. This is what we mean by network. What can they bring to the table to help the TWO of you build a mutually rewarding business?

Let me share a personal example with you. I recruited a middle-aged fellow who was a failed dentist. His name was Reggie. Now, Reggie tried to 'like' being a dentist, but he hated the profession and quit. He was broke, had a large debt from his education and was under pressure to get a job from his wife.

Now, Reggie hated the idea of getting a 'job'. So he searched ads and saw one of mine, 'why take a job when you can be making money instead' – something like that. (FYI – this ad was in a weekly local paper, which still work!).

He came straight over to meet me at a local coffee shop. He wore a very ill-fitting suit and did not look 'in shape' by any means. However, he had a great smile. I did a one-on-one presentation for him and got him a coffee. He was 'in' right away but he was broke and could not even purchase any product, let alone a second cup of java. However, I lent him some products (which I don't recom-mend in general but something about Reggie told me that his willingness to work would be worth more money to me than a first-time product order – I watched as he was jotting down names on a piece of paper without being asked).

Now, Reggie knew a few people in his church - which was the center of his life. It was not like he was 'using' his connections there – his church was very social and no one looked down on anyone who spoke about non-church related topics. Everyone there spoke about spiritual, business and social issues. He later told me everyone at his church had a very high level of self-esteem, and no one would complain about bringing 'outside-life' into church – and making money is a good part of life!).

Reggie loved our networking concept and his love showed – so people were attracted to listening to him and wanted to find out what got him so excited.

On his list was a fellow church goer – a middle aged man who owned a place-ment agency, (if you needed a job as an office temp his company would find you one). He was already a multi-millionaire, drove a Porsche, and had a big mansion and some nice downtown offices. His name was Pascal.

Of course you can see that sponsoring someone like Pascal who had these resources would be extraordinary. He had money, influence, connections, and was already successful. So I told Reggie to definitely keep Pascal on his list.

Reggie was a little concerned by Pascal's success – after all – why would he want to join our network company? He was already successful and wealthy, 'why should we approach him?'

I told Reggie not to think about that –I'll explain why later; for now let's just do our job and show him our business.

We went to see Pascal in his plush downtown office. I'm not sure why, but his PA was very snooty. However Pascal himself was genuinely happy to see us. As we entered his office he asked his snooty PA to bring us some coffee. He really wanted to know what had Reggie so excited.

Within 30 minutes we had done a two-on-one presentation.   Pascal was interested and excited too. We agreed to have a coffee together after our next live-meeting at a local hotel. Long story short, Pascal joined up, used his office, his contacts, and some spare office space to set up a co-op and start his own meetings. That one leg earned me well over $5-9K per month for years, and even more for Reggie.

You see? We sought Pascal because we knew he had resources and contacts. We tapped into them. He earned about 10K per month very quickly, and soon he was hitting $25K.

FYI Pascal did NOT prospect anyone listed with his placement agency. Besides the conflict of interest, he told said they were 'not success profiles...'

Now, some people would not have tried to recruit a successful rich business person. After all, why would someone rich and successful join us?

What's in it for them? Fair question.

Well, our reason for recruiting him was simple - because of his resources and contacts. Of course he could have said no, but that's not the point. Because as it's our job to tap in to someone else's network we chose to present our business to him.

If he said 'no' so what?

So why are so many networkers 'afraid' to talk to prospects like Pascal?

The real reason is this:

We assume that because they have what we don't – the outward trappings of success – that they don't need what we offer. But by avoiding these people we are saying 'no' for them.

Yet, we are networkers – our job is to present to those with resources and connections that we don't have so that we may tap into them.

So why do so many people NOT present to their doctors, lawyers, or other outwardly 'successful' people?

Well, sometimes it's poor-self-esteem, 'not wanting to present to our 'betters', but I don't want to get into psychology here. There is a far simpler reason: we forget that money is not the only reason to become involved in networking.

Money is not the only gratification there is.

For many it is money, but for others it's very different.

In Pascal's case it was this: That business of his was established by his father. Pascal married a woman that his father had approved of and was wealthy herself too. He never had to strive for anything, and never 'chose' the job of running the job-placement agency. It was given to him. We did not know this before we presented to him. He only told us after.

He was what we call a 'dis-satisfied success'.

This is when I told Reggie about how I recruited my first doctor.

I was new to networking, perhaps about 5 months at it. I was earning about 4 to 6K a month, depending on the month. I worked hard and presented to people each day. One day one of my downline asked if I would do a two-on-one with his Doctor at the medical center where the Doctor worked.

I was a bit unsure if it would be worth it, 'why would a Doctor want to do this?' I asked myself, but to my team-member I said 'sure, happy to do it.' I knew my job was to make presentations, so even if this was a waste of time, my job was to present, and it would look good to my guy.

Well, the day came and we went to see the Doctor in his office.

I was nervous as heck, and would have welcomed any excuse not to go. I could not wait for the Doctor to say 'no' so we could get back to looking for 'real prospects'.

Things started to be uncomfortable as soon as we walked into the office. His receptionist looked down on us with a smirk. I think sometimes the 'hired help' tend to take on the social status of those they work for – whereas those they work for are usually just 'regular folks'. Weird.

After having to wait for 20 minutes we were allowed in to see him. He was quiet. He sat down, looking bored let me start. When I was finished he asked some questions, but without any real enthusiasm.

He agreed to come to a Saturday morning meeting, where we did a short presentation and then a 'training' at a local hotel.

He actually arrived that Saturday morning early!

I lost a bet with myself – I felt sure he'd be a no-show.

By the end of the training that Saturday he signed up and placed his first big product purchase.   I was not his direct sponsor, but wanted me to be his mentor, so I agreed.

He told me he hated his practice, that he was over-worked, trapped by mortgages, cars, kids in university, and paying for a big life style.

There was no way out. That's why he looked 'bored' in his office. Because he was so tired that he did not have the energy to show his feelings. He later told me that he had been 'over the moon excited' but just did not have one drop of stamina left that day.

As months went on, he build a leg that would earn me 10k per month.

So, you see, our job – is to make presentations – to Doctors, Lawyers, or homemakers, or anyone in order to tap into their list or resources. We don't say 'no' for folks. We let them say no.

My attitude was not great back then – I was convinced that the Doctor was not going to be interested, especially as we sat under the 'evil eye' of his receptionist.

Of course that was a long time ago.

My mindset was very different.

But what else was different was my experience.

So you see, I made those presentations to Pascal and to the doctor because we knew they had contacts. Because it is our job as networkers to tap into their resources.

My Attitude was not great – I was convinced that the doctor was not going to be interested. And as for Pascal, Reggie's attitude was to not call Pascal because Pascal was already successful.

But my Mindset (not Attitude) was perfect. My Mindset was *'my job is to make presentations to those who have resources and contacts that I don't have. It's not to make them say 'yes', or to say 'no' for them – it's just to present'.*

I was still nervous (that's attitude) but my mindset was 100%.

You see?

That leads us to the next step in creating the perfect Mindset for networking, your DMO.

The Secret of Achieving Perfect Mindset – Just Three Little Letters

Your DMO or Daily Method of Operation

What must we do in order to work past a poor or negative Attitude?

And I'll admit my Attitude – even today - is not always 'perfect'. Oh boy, NOT AT ALL!!! Our emotions are not always ours to command.

But Mindset is not emotional – and therefore we do control it. Our mindset is ours to command.

The person who tells you that they have perfect control over their Attitude is lying to themselves.

But it doesn't matter. Because it's not Attitude that determines your Altitude; (but it's a cute saying and it rhymes nicely). It's your Mindset. If denying 'Attitude is all' sounds like an unpardonable sin, just read on, and you'll understand. I'll bet your attitude is pretty darn good anyway!

By the way: Once our Mindset is under control, your Attitude will catch up as best as it can. But even after you have hit $10K or higher per month – you will have periods of 'bad' Attitude. So if you control you Mindset you will hit the $10K plus per month and you can worry about your Attitude in style.

Of course a good attitude is better than a bad one – but as you read you'll begin to realize that Mindset is more important.

So, what's Mindset all about?

Simple: Mindset is all about time and what you do with it. **Key**

The two key words in that sentence are Time and DO.

This is where our DMO comes in, our 'Daily Method of Operation'.

And it's a very strict daily Method of Operation too. That means time is more precious than anything else. We'll get to the 'strict' part later when we analyze the type of 'boss' you are.

First, let's analyze our time.

After all, time is all we have.

Our job is to use our time wisely. If you are being 'active' and not 'productive', you are wasting your time. If you are not engaged in a smart prospecting method for one reason or another, then you are not going to find success. And worse, you are wasting your time.

Not only your time. You're robbing your family of the time you could be spending with them because you are not being productive in the time you think you are spending on your business.

This is important: When you are just active and not productive, you are stealing from others as well as yourself.

Remember, we all have loved ones. We make an agreement with them: 'Let me work on and in this new business. Sometimes I'll be on the phone, sometimes away at meetings, sometimes I'll go away for a weekend convention – but please support me and know that I am doing it so later I can spend more time with you.'

That is an agreement. Sometimes it's spoken, sometimes it's unspoken.

But it's a contract or agreement just the same.

However we break our agreement if we are only 'being active' or looking busy, getting ready to get ready', or spending endless hours on the web 'researching,' or speaking to people who have already been sponsored. That is not being productive.

Once we understand that it's our family's time we are stealing when we are not working the business properly, a lot becomes clear. We begin to see our time from a different perspective. This is time they willingly gave us and if we abuse that time, we are stealing from them.

We will be creating a written personal contract later in the book – I just wanted you to get introduced to the concept here. We are in business and each player in business has a contract. You'll have one soon.

What's your PI Level?

What's your Personal Integrity Level? High, medium, or worse?

We are talking about personal integrity. To yourself and your family.

You can fool the family by being active but you can't fool yourself. You know if you are productive or just 'active'.

And one day you will quit the business and say, "It didn't work."

It's easy to lie to yourself.

It's better to quit now than to shoulder a huge burden of guilt if you are just going to be playing at the business.

I would rather have someone who is productive 3 hours per week – part time – than someone who is active 40 hours per week but productive only 10.

The 40 hour 'full-timer' will NOT make enough money to support themselves - at only 10 productive hours per week. Instead, they will quit, be unhappy, blame their upline, downline, the economy, Congress, their company, their products, the prices of their products, the color of the box the products are sent in, or any other silly reason they can make up to avoid admitting it was their lack of productivity that was the reason for their failure.

You can't just go into your home-office or bedroom and stare at the phone or your laptop.

You need to DO.

How do we make 'Doing' easier and effective?

Through our DMO. Daily Method Operation

Once you see this clearly and follow a DMO, you will watch your income rise along with your Attitude. I guarantee it.

Once you engage and follow your DMO - of doing what needs to be done by being productive not active, you will create income.

It's time to be productive. It's time to establish your daily method of operation. And as I said, it's a *strict* daily method of operation!

What is the DMO killer?

To understand what stops us from adopting the Mindset of production and following our DMO and taking action, let's look at the reverse, what is it that drives us to change, to get out of our comfort zone?

Simple - dissatisfaction.

When we don't change, even if we think we want to, it's because there's not enough dissatisfaction with the way things are.

We need dissatisfaction for growth or business growth.

This is why we constantly hear 'get out of your comfort zone' in training after training. There really is a very strong attachment in our genes toward staying in our comfort zone.

It goes back to mankind's earliest days. When things were good, we stayed put and didn't go off exploring - those that did often didn't come back.

We are programmed to be lazy. Our genes program us to save calories, to park our cars at the nearest door to the mall.

Have you ever wondered why we are so lazy?

It may sound funny, but it's not: it's our genetic programming to save calories. To do as little as possible. This is why it's hard to lose weight; we are programmed to reach for calories and to not expend them unless it's a life or death matter.

It's only in the last 150 years that we have access to cheap, unhealthy calorie-laden foods and a lifestyle where we don't have to get up and be active to earn a living.

Our programming was designed to help us by saving calories as a reserve to use in times of trouble.

This served us well until food became more plentiful, carbohydrate-rich, wages increased, and technology started to make life so easy that we all got fat.

Side Note: If you have a 'home-office body – get out and take a walk each day!

Our genetic programming is not changing as fast as technology has progressed.

It's important to know that this programming is in all of us. I struggle with it myself every day. So do you, so do your prospects and your downline.

We can't change how we are programmed – but we can change our Mindset to take action, which brings us back to our DMO.

Make no mistake - change is not comfortable at first – but it becomes far more comfortable later. You can thank your programming for that too. We are also programed to make doing what we don't like to do easier and easier with each repetition. The more you perform an action the better and better you get at it – and the result is that it saves time and energy.

The good news is this: no matter what you don't like doing or are not good at performing you will get better with each repetition - and that will make you feel better about doing it!

How to turn Addiction into Action

Remember the days when you were a network newbie?

Think about the person you have just sponsored. You and I both know that they can drop out very quickly. We all know about the critical first 48 hours.

Let me tell you about one of my former lawyers, and how she joined my team.

I had a pretty good real estate lawyer and I went to her for a new real estate deal. I met her a few times in her fancy office regarding a house I was buying and at the time I was pretty young. She asked me how I got the money to afford another house and I just went into presentation mode. Now this was back before laptops were powerful enough for serious presentations - but I had a color copy of our PowerPoint presentation in my binder. I spread it across her desk without a second's hesitation.

After I showed her our plan, my binder opened to page after page of color photocopies of my income checks, (back before direct deposit was mandatory I would insist the company send me paper checks – in those days we were still allowed to show income!).

I pushed the binder closer to her to see if she would flip the pages herself and look at all my checks. They were monthly – she looked at each of them, more and more amazed as she flipped. They were from my first checks to my latest – meaning they got progressively higher!

I said, "Hey, if you'd like to see how that kind of income is made why not come to our presentation tomorrow."

She arrived on time – and with her brother. I sat them down in the front row and I watched them from where I stood, (I was one of the presenters).

As soon as the meeting ended, I got swamped by downline and their prospects. I could only get a short glimpse of my lawyer and her brother. I saw him nod his head quickly to her and then take off like a bolt of lightning.

After a few minutes, I was able to sit beside her and she said 'we're in', at the $6K level. "Pick up a check tomorrow."

She and her brother signed up. I told her about the training on the following Saturday and left her with all the kit, manuals, etc.

She missed Saturday's training.

I called and left messages on both their phones.

As my real estate deal was all done, I had no reason to visit her office again but I kept calling her about getting trained.

She finally called me back and said she was very sorry but really did not have much time for 'this'. She asked if I could just stop calling her until she called me.

Well, I earned over $1000 on that product order, but that was not the point. It's a waste of time to NOT get her resources – and some activity from a new person. I knew she could have done well.

Her reason, she later told me, was that she was 'unconformable' talking to her business colleagues. "What would they think?" It made her uncomfortable.

I told her, "There is little comfortable in earning the income that I earn –if you want to earn income like this you must be willing to get uncomfortable."

She never returned the product, or ever called me upset about the money she spent. I think she felt like she let me down.

Well she DID let me down.

Now I know you'll say, "No, she let herself down."

Well, that's true of course.

But she let me down too. I work hard and care about what I do. If someone joins me I plan to work with them and assist them to earn a lot of money – because I will too. I'm not looking for the one-time commission on an order.

I didn't become a network marketer for one time sales income. I am here for the residuals.

But the point is this: if she, you, or I, are unwilling to ditch our comfort zone from time to time, day to day, week in and week out, nothing will change.

We must become 'uncomfortable' to change and acquire wealth.

If you're wondering where the pleasure is if you're always uncomfortable – I can tell you that too. It comes from those little endorphins that are released in our brain at the moment of accomplishment. And you only get that accomplishment from something done outside your comfort zone. It's a wonderful feeling!

Each time you break free of your comfort-zone there is immense pleasure. Yet we had to become 'uncomfortable' to get that pleasure.

The greater the accomplishment the greater the feeling of pleasure and pride in ourselves.

It gets addicting – in a good way.

So with discomfort comes reward.

There is the reward you feel when your family, your children, your spouse – see you cross the stage having achieved a new position, being acknowledged by the company president, being presented with that big cardboard check or a new pin to the applause of the entire conference hall.

To feel the pride in those moments is a big reward and only comes with being 'uncomfortable'.

And last and not least: the money comes. Once it starts coming in regularly it is less rewarding than the admiration of your peers and family.

Now, to continue our understanding of how to change our Mindset, let's finish the story of my lawyer.

She is like a lot of your prospects and your downline and to be honest like a lot of us.

She was dissatisfied with her income - and when she saw mine she desired it. The money, not the work, just the money.

Once she saw the work – she retreated back into her world faster than a Lamborghini.

Her Attitude was this, "If I feel I can manage it, I'm going to hang on to my present situation. I'm going to hang onto it and then hope for the best. I want comfort more than change."

Yet we know that there is something missing from her world. Clearly there is not enough money, or she would not have been looking at my checks with desire. Sadly for her what was the fact that her feeling of 'lack' – of more money - was not as painful as her willingness to become uncomfortable.

I'm sure you have had downline that quit – sometimes after a few days, a few weeks or a few months. They told you they 'tried, really tried'. But as soon as they experienced any discomfort – or even the thought of it – that's when they quit. No matter what excuse they told you – it was all about them – not you – not your company – not your pay plan – or any other reason. The reason was all in their mirror.

Obviously, if people are ineffective in their efforts and are unwilling to get uncomfortable there is no gratification or reward. Those folks are just wasting their time, your time and lying to themselves.

But for those of us who honestly desire change and are willing to get uncomfortable about it, the method is the Mindset of action by following a strict DMO.

Don't worry about learning skills first, because by following your DMO you will repeat actions and learn the skills that go with it. Over a matter of repetitions you will become more effective and become more productive. More effective means more results and that means momentum, gratification and income!

Let me introduce you to your current DMO – Even if you don't think you have one

A strategic plan is the term we use to describe the final goal for our DMO. Think of it as your long-term goal.

Our day-to-day activity is called our DMO, or Daily Method of Operation. It leads us to successfully reach our strategic goal, (think of your DMO as a list of tactics broken down by task).

So what is your plan? What is the desired outcome of your DMO?

You know – your strategic plan for wealth or income?

Perhaps you believe you don't have one?

But you do.

Let's look at it this way.

If I we were driving to Denver from Las Vegas, and we were taking the I-70, you could say our strategic plan was to get to Denver.

What if we noticed someone on the I-70 heading towards Denver following us?

When we pulled over for gas, so did they. So let's get out and talk to them. We ask them where they are headed.

"Hey, we're not really sure. We noticed you have a nice car and you folks seem to be enjoying the drive, so we just decided to follow you for a while."

Even when we think we don't have a strategic plan we're following something or someone – even if we don't know it or know why. So that becomes the plan – it's just not our plan.

What you do each day IS the plan you are following.

Perhaps it changes day to day! A surefire method to get no-place.

This is true for your current business life, and your personal and family life.

This is where most of us get lost.

We are following someone else's plan and we don't even know it. We are just going along for the ride.

Often this is where networkers complain they get confused by hearing different methods to do the business. Some people believe in online leads, some – like me J - preach direct mail, some 3 foot rule, others do resumes. There are lots of effective lead generation methods. Not only one. The problem for people without a plan is that they try different plans out for a day or a week and don't see any results. No plan will work that fast. Then they blame their upline for exposing them to different and confusing lead generation methods.

I am biased against 'online purchased leads' but I know people who do very well with them. I love direct mail, and offline lead generation, but I also love online follow up. But that is my plan. My plan is not the only plan. I know people who earn a very substantial income just using LinkedIn. Some that just use Face-book.

Some still are using ads in USAToday successfully.

There are many more methods. But you must pick one of them and follow it. That will determine the actions within your DMO.

(FYI – you can use more than one method at a time – but make sure they mesh – you can't be out all day doing the '3 foot rule' at Starbucks AND do online leads at the same time).

Try this thought experiment: Pretend that someone would follow you each day for a week watching you do the business and recorded what your actions - and at the end those 7 days, they gave you a detailed report.

That's your DMO. Most likely that DMO will not lead you to any place you want to be.

So, it's far better to choose your own strategic plan that is effective FOR YOU and will take you to your goals.

NB: for those who say 'I want the method that makes the most money in the fastest way – like 'so-and-so' top-producer. Be willing to take the time it takes to REALLY learn how she or he works that system – because you will not learn it in a week – even if someone tells you that you can.

We have two options:

One - we can continue to follow our ineffective DMO - which basically means having no plan, just hanging around, hoping for things to happen or hoping somebody shows up and joins our team and is an instant success – like winning the MLM lottery. Or, maybe someone in our upline will promise, "If you just hang in there and stay on autoship, you will eventually make money." So we hang on to that promise so we can blame our upline later when we learn that just staying on autoship doesn't cut it.

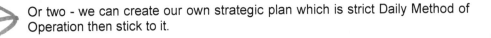

Or two - we can create our own strategic plan which is strict Daily Method of Operation then stick to it.

Mindset – Stage 1 - Implementation

Setting up and implementing our DMO is simple and straight forward.

It means setting out the answers to the following questions, and then following that plan.

The 6 Questions for us as network marketers are these:

1. Who
2. What
3. When
4. Where
5. Why
6. How

1. Who are you going to contact?
2. What are we going to say?
3. When are we going to do it?
4. Where are we going to do it?
5. Why we're going to do it?
6. How are we going to do it?

We must have that implementation in place.

What is in your DMO?

First you need to identify what you need to do each 'work day'.

What's a work day? Only you can decide, but once you decide, consider it a matter of personal integrity to stick to it. Think how MUCH time you can dedicate to reaching your goal – not how LITTLE!

Make your prospecting and follow up calls in a certain time slot and stick to that time slot.

Make note about how many quality conversations you make. Start now using that term – 'quality conversations' instead of making note of how many calls you make – which included people who didn't want to talk to you. From now on it's only quality conversations that count. Those other conversations are not productive. Sure it's a call but we are looking for quality conversations.

For example, my goal was 10 quality conversations a day. 10 calls that I would connect with someone and explain what I've got and engage them into my recruiting system. Your company has some kind of recruiting system too. Our job is to put people through that system, and a quality conversation is putting someone in that system and following up with them after.

In my case I found that 10 quality conversations would lead to 3 long term prospects and 3 'hot' prospects. Typically I would convert 1 prospect out of 10. Sometimes much more, but your rations will depend on repetition – gaining skills, lead quality and your exposure system. Keep tinkering with your system until you find your numbers are at their maximum. When people are not happy with their numbers they get frustrated. Me too. But tinker with your system, numbers and DMO until it works. Those who don't deserve to be in our industry will instead quit. But not you. I mean that sincerely.

FYI: a quality call is not calling your upline or downline, it's a call with prospects.

If you're working with a new person, speaking with their prospects is a quality call, provided it means a direct income for you. Otherwise it's a support call, which you must do too, but it does not get included in your total quality conversation count.

Now, perhaps 10 is not the right number for you, perhaps its 15, 20, (or 7 or 3). Hey, it's up to you – but once you choose your number, stick to it. Eventually you'll know your rations of actions > to prospects > to new sign-ups.

Of course if you are part-time or have a different situation you must decide on your numbers – make them realistic to reach your goal, but not impossible with the time you have available.

NOTE: A DMO is just your list of Daily (income producing) Activities – it's small enough that most people write it out and tape it to the wall in front of them. It may be just a list, but it's a powerful tool in the MLM world.

Note

How we avoid lying to ourselves:

Just following your DMO is not the whole process. The other essential part of your DMO is tracking your other activities. We record this in a business diary or journal.

What goes in your business journal?

What did you do today?

Write a short sentence or paragraph of our overall business day. Ideas, observations, people that were worth remembering, things that worked, what didn't, etc.

Next come the numbers:

- How many quality conversations?
- How many 3-way calls?
- How many training actions did you listen to that day?
- Which ones? Note how these trainings directly answered a need in you, or a lack in you.

Start noting what areas of training you need to zero in on. I know your upline will say to be on every call, but you need to start choosing the training you need. Too many times we avoid work by listening to trainings that we don't need.

Start listing what training your team needs and either set up a time so you can do a group training conference call or webinar, or, find an upline who is more qualified and able.

We all need training, but ask yourself this – what do you need more – 10 more distributors in your team or more training? Time-effective networkers record calls or listen to recorded training calls during non-prospecting hours.

Revisit your journal often by keeping it open and handy. Make a note with each call or action – soon you'll start enjoying seeing the numbers increase.

With one glance you'll know the state of the nation of your business.

I like to keep track of everything. This is what the pro's do. You can be a pro by starting this process and sticking to it!

When someone joins, be sure to record that in your journal too– start noticing how long it took for someone to start as a prospect and end up being a 'no' or a new member. Keep track of these statistics on a separate page too. Soon you will see that it becomes faster for you to find out if someone is a real prospect or just a 'tire-kicker'.

If you are a computer-prone person, Onenote by Microsoft is pretty good to use to build a diary, but if you don't have it, or don't want to learn how to use it, just get started with a journal that you can pick up at the office supply store in your town.

Onenote is pretty simple, and there are many YouTube videos explaining it.

FYI: There are plenty of simple online diary programs that are private – that you can use too. Don't get blogged down trying to decide which one to use, just pick one and get started.

Personally I recommend a spiral notebook. Not just because my mentors used them and so did the founders of our industry (some of them used hardbound notebooks too), but because they are lite, easy to carry, and they lay flat on your desk.

If you keep focusing on the actions that get you 'productivity', i.e., quality conversations - you will soon find that you have launched yourself into momentum.

I can guarantee you will get into momentum if you take action using your personalized Daily Method of Operation.

In over 20 years of networking, I have some experience. I'm not saying I'm smarter than others – I'm not. But smarter is not always a guarantee of success. However practical experience is something I have!

By focusing on my DMO, my productivity went straight up and close behind it my momentum. As a result my income went up, and THEN my Attitude changed! I got 'happy' with doing follow-up calls - something I did not enjoy before.

You see? Creating a DMO is not hard at all, it's not difficult, you don't need to see anyone else's, (it will only confuse you), just make note of your actions.

NOTE: if you are doubtful of your actions it just means you don't have a set method for lead generation and putting people through your 'system'. My other books focus on lead generation methods, and your company will no doubt have a 'system' in place for you to process your leads.

FREE OFFER:

If you would like a sample DMO and Journal Entry for a business diary, just email me at DavidWilliamsMLMAuthor@gmail.com and put DMO Sample in the subject line.

Mindset – Stage 2 - the Contract

Once you have your implementation stage settled, in other words decided on what you must do to reach your goals, you need to be accountable to yourself. So you need to make a personal contract.

It's all about integrity.

We often forget that we must act with integrity to ourselves as well as to others.

If you promise something to yourself and then deliver it - even when you don't feel like it – you are acting with 'personal integrity.'

Your personal contract is just as important as making a contract with anyone else.

And note well: if you fail to deliver on your personal contract you'll learn not to trust yourself. Once you don't trust yourself you enter into a whole world of challenges that we don't have space to address here!

NOTE: if you find you keep braking your networking personal contract it maybe that you have been unrealistic in your time management – lower your numbers until you are able to keep your personal commitment and begin to raise them as you are able. Don't create a giant goal that you have no realistic hope of achieving right away; your DMO must make sense to your time available. This is why you don't want your upline setting your goals for you, often or not they will create unrealistically high goals for you that are really designed to have you reach THEIR goals. At the same time, if you find you are not 'stretching' or getting out of your comfort zone, you must raise that bar too. You are wise and intelligent so balance out your DMO between your goals, desires, ability, and your time.

When you fulfill your contract to yourself it means one important thing: you have integrity and you delivered what you promised.

You will feel good about that. You made a contract with yourself and you delivered on it.

That is personal leadership and integrity.

This business is all about personal leadership and integrity.

Action Exercise:

Make a contract with yourself. If you respect yourself you'll deliver on it. Get in the habit of doing this - make personal contracts a habit and you'll be amazed at what you accomplish. That habit will soon enhance your professional and personal life.

FREE OFFER

If you would like a sample Contract for Networkers, just email me at DavidWilliamsMLMAuthor@gmail.com and put Networking Contract in the subject line and I'll send one to you!

You don't need to marry a psychiatrist to learn how suspending your DMO is crazy...

Let me tell you about one young man I sponsored in a nearby city. His story provides us some great lessons – about management mode, tracking, the costly habit of lying to ourselves – and how the best of intentions can destroy our Mindset.

I placed an ad in the local PennySaver - it was a high-income advertisement. Something like '10K per month if you enjoy public speaking – call for details'.

I had just sponsored a friend of mine and I told him I was going to get this nearby city going. His wife did not have a job and they were empty nesters so I suggested he pay for an ad, and his wife take the calls. All I told her to say was that anyone interested was to show up at the Howard Johnston's where we held our meetings. She was too new to learn anything else at that time. This is not a great way of doing the business, but I wanted to make use of their resources: her time at home and willingness to answer the phone live.

Meanwhile, this young guy, Ben, was working as a sales clerk in an art supply shop. His bored co-workers were reading the classifieds in the PennySaver for entertainment and spotted my ad.

"Hey Ben, you're always talking about making it big, here, call this number."

So Ben did call and spoke to my friend's wife. For whatever reason he decided to attend our meeting.

(Ben later told me that he only came because the Howard Johnston's was on his way home.)

But by the end of the presentation Ben was 'in'. He joined right away, and that leg took off.

Within a few months he was at $10K, and later hitting $30K per month.

It takes high performance obviously - which is what launched him into momentum.

However 20 months later Ben hit an income/production valley due to a poor decision he made. He decided to ONLY 'help' his team instead of sponsoring.

In networking we call it taking your foot off the gas —eventually your engine coasts to a stop. It's also known as 'management mode'. "I have hit it big, now I'm going to take time to work with my team to 'help' them."

I took Ben aside when he first told me of his 'I'm going to stop sponsoring so I can help my team' plan.

I knew this was trouble.

I asked him what one of the main philosophies we teach in our industry?

He said a few things, but when he hit on 'duplication', I stopped him.

I said, "If you stop sponsoring to 'help your team', won't your team see that and also duplicate what you do too?"

"Oh no," says he, "Because I'm making $20K per month. Once they are earning that then they will duplicate me."

I told him, "Just watch what happens."

Ben changed his DMO. He stopped looking for quality conversations, stopped prospecting, and started 'working with his people'.

Ben was a good leader, very personable and his team liked and followed him.

That was the problem.

All his top people stopped prospecting, and started 'working with their team' too - just like Ben. It spread like a cancer throughout his team.

Everyone was willing to 'help' their downline.

But nothing got done.

Helping your downline means either training as a group or you being part of the process, (like doing a 3-way call, providing social proof, testimonials, small house presentations, etc.). When someone is new, it's also closing for your new team member.

But when you 'force' help on your team, it usually is just 'motivational' talks, coffees, calls, chit-chat, etc. And you tend to focus on the worse performers you have - and they don't even have any prospects.

Ben's income sagged down to less than $7K.

He got worried. Scared.

So he got back in the trenches and started working again.

But guess what?

Ben, a consistent high earner now couldn't sponsor anyone.

Ben didn't sponsor anyone the entire month - he started losing his confidence. "After all," he thought, "I'm calling all of these people but nobody wants to sign up. Maybe something is wrong with our business."

You see, our natural behavior is to blame something or somebody else rather than ourselves.

When we don't achieve what we want in this industry, the problem is always in the mirror.

Remember that. It's always in the mirror. You can blame your sponsor all day long. But if you do, you're not going to find success.

Whatever your goal is, you're not going to achieve it by blaming someone else. You won't have a big month if you blame your upline or your downline, or your parents or your pastor or husband or wife.

Instead you let go of blame and you take responsibility - you say to yourself, "Let me change something in my action, not my Attitude, and see what happens."

What happened to Ben?

After a full 6 weeks of Ben's business falling in income, he came to meet me. That meant driving an hour to my city – something he never liked doing. But I told him to come and to bring his business journal. Back then, we used over-sized day-timers – it's not because we didn't have laptops – it was just faster to make written notes.

(I'm still not convinced that writing notes isn't better.)

Ben bought lunch and asked me, "So what's going on? Something has happened to the business, I can't get anyone good to a meeting, and no one wants
to talk to me...is there something you haven't told me?"

I calmly finished my desert and told him to wait until the table was cleared.

He was someone who – had he been asked – would have known what was
wrong. The challenge is that we are pretty good in judging others but poor in
judging ourselves. Psychiatrists go to other psychiatrists. They know you can't
figure yourself out.

So in Ben's case, I asked him to 'show me'.

 "What?"

I told him to show me his business journal for his best month.

He opened his book and looked up his best month. I had him count the number
of quality conversations he had in total. It was pretty easy for him, because each
of my team leaders kept count of their DMO actions each day.

It was approximately 10 quality conversations per day, or 200 per month.

I asked him to make a note of that number on the paper napkin, remembering
Big Al's famous book.

Next, I asked him to count the number of his quality conversations in the last full
month, the one where he had seen his worst income.

He told me it would be 'about the same', that he had 'done the same work' - that
he had 'worked just as hard'.

But I told him to humor me and count them anyway.

When he finished counting his face paled.

He flipped thought page after page, muttering, "That can't be right...I must have
forgot to write anything on that day...oh my, I don't believe it."

He made only 17 quality conversations.

In a month.

But in his mind, he thought he had done the same work as he had months ago.

"Ben," I said, "It's all about the numbers. Just go back to 200 per month AND DO THEM and you'll find your month is much better. Nothing has changed in the company, the economy, so Ben, the only difference is your action. Forget that you have some worries – or don't forget – I don't care. Just do your numbers and watch. The magic is in the numbers, nothing else."

Two months later Ben had his second highest month ever and never went back into management mode again. Today he's happily married to a psychiatrist. She never asks him to get a 'real job'.

You see, when our results are poor we tend to think we are doing the same DMO when in fact we are not. We think we are working harder than we are.

That's why it's so important to track what you are doing. Track your feelings too. Track how you felt about certain situations. Just because it's a business diary, don't forget to make a note of how you feel. For example, "Today I tried doing 15 quality conversations and I did! I feel great, not tired, but very proud of myself. I can't wait until tomorrow to start again!"

If you trust yourself, you will record everything in your own personal business diary. If you do this, you will be able to re-create the same conditions by going back into a diary and rereading it – it gives you a nice way to quickly get back into the mental groove of winning. It's not essential, but you might as well do it.

Right now, without a business diary or journal, you can't trust your feelings or memory. You need to see the numbers because the numbers don't lie.

Until you adopt this practice, you don't know where you are. You think you are doing the same thing as you did in your best week or month, but don't believe it until you can see it in black and white.

For Ben, he thought he was doing the same amount of income producing activities – and maybe he was or maybe he wasn't – but until we opened the book nothing was known. Without looking at his numbers he got negative - everything he saw would reinforced his negativity.

So track your numbers - that's one of the most important parts of your DMO – it's not just DOING that's important – it's just as important to track your numbers.

Mindset is doing – your DMO is the simple list of what you must do on a daily basis.

If you think you are self-employed you are not using the right Mindset

How many times have you heard to treat networking as a business?

But too many networkers consider themselves as self-employed.

There is a Mindset difference between being self-employed and running a business.

If you run a business you are the boss.

If you are self-employed you don't have a boss.

Just for the fun answer, read the following scenarios:

Monday:

It's just 11:30 a.m. You just had a new distributor sign up and place a qualifying order. This person has been in the loop for 3 weeks and has lots of good experience – no doubt they are going to be a good leg. You deserve to take the rest of the day off. After all we work for ourselves so there better be some perks!

Wednesday:

You log into your bank account and notice you have earned a bigger bonus than you expected. Enough to get a new car! You hop in your old jalopy and take the day off to go car shopping – you'll be able to give your team a great story about your new car, motivating them.

Friday:

One of your key team players calls you. Her husband won the lottery so they're quitting the business and moving to the south of France. You're happy for them - but you realize that will mean you'll lose a good producer, and there will be a loss of momentum. It's hard to make prospecting calls when you feel like that, so you deserve a little me-time and that's best done by a spa day or playing golf.

So here's the question.

If you had a 'boss' and the same events occurred, would your boss believe you should take time off for doing your job right? For sponsoring someone? Or would your boss tell you 'great, take that victory and get back to your prospecting, you'll only inspire more people.'

With that unexpected bonus would your boss tell you to "Get out of here, and go buy a new car! Don't wait until your prospecting time is over – take off now, you deserve it!" Or would your boss tell you, "I'm happy you're buying a new car with that bonus, the others will admire it and work harder after they see yours. I know most car dealers are open in non-productive hours. We'll look forward to hearing all about your new car on our next call!"

Lastly, if you lost a big deal, would your boss tell you to "Get out of here, go to a movie, play some golf or to the spa and shake it off?" Or would they say, "Look, the only thing to do is get back on your horse. People come and go in the business each day – you can't take a day off each time it happens."

Ask yourself, who is the better boss?

The one that lets you off early, or the one that keeps you tied to your personal contract?

This is what we mean when we say, "All distractions are equal."

Good distractions – like a big bonus – or bad ones – like the loss of a distributor.

A good boss is one who does NOT let you slack off when you are victim to a bad Attitude – nor will he or she allow you to slack off because you did what you were paid to do – sponsor someone.

Not if you have a contract.

Not if you have integrity.

Especially if you've promised your family that you're really going to make this work, and work harder than you would at a 'job'.

If you follow the slacker boss that is a Mindset mistake.

You are a business. You must monitor and track your employees – and that's YOU.

If you miss this step you don't deserve to be in business, and the free market will toss you out of business very quickly.

You see it happen in our industry everyday – and those who let it happen to themselves will blame you if you are their sponsor or the company or the products or the prices or the compensation plan. And when they hang up the phone after telling you they quit, you can bet they don't go near the mirror – because few are willing to face the truth.

And speaking about the 'truth' this was one of my biggest personal lessons. You see, I would reward myself right away after a victory, thinking that was motivating to do so. Or I would shake off a setback by taking a break also thinking that was the right thing to do. It was when I learned to continue with my DMO – victory or set-back – that I made a major leap in my income and begin to understand the power of Mindset.

OKAY – so what's MY DMO?

As this book is not centered on any specific method or company, each of us will have a slightly different DMO. Some people use live meetings, send samples, use postcards, voice mail messages, video webinars, conference calls, etc, etc. Depending on what you use you need to track these things in your business diary and use them to set up your DMO.

Each of us - depending on the company we are working with – and even within the same company – will have a different series of exposures for recruiting and prospecting. Some of us will have more than one series of exposures depending on the different lead generation methods we us. But that's for advanced prospecting, and usually for full-timers. If that's you – you'll understand and adjust your DMO to reflect that.

However, in general you will have one series of exposures for your prospecting and recruiting.

Just a reminder, if you would like a sample DMO and Journal Entry for a business diary, just email me at DavidWilliamsMLMAuthor@gmail.com and put DMO Sample in the subject line.

Do a final review of your running total at the end of the night, and do some comparisons at that time, or early in the morning, depending on your lifestyle. Either way, crunch your numbers – your daily object is to try and beat your record, or at least your numbers the day before, until it becomes impossible.

That's when you know you're successful - as your bank account will be telling you.

It's at this time that 'MLM' becomes easy. You're so busy - and you love it.

Reminder: Your DMO is not a BIG deal to write. But don't let its size fool you. It should be small enough for you to write on a recipe/index card (old school) and tape it up in your home office where you can see it as your go through the steps on a daily basis.

Want to see my personal DMO Demo?

One evening I was doing a conference call training about the DMO with my team.

I shared my own DMO and my numbers with everyone. "My goal," I said, "Is at least 10 quality conversations each working day. Now I only can speak about me, I can't speak about somebody else's life, as some folks have 5 young kids, or single parents, etc, etc."

So here I was just about to close the training call, when I made this unplanned offer to my team. I said, "If anybody wants to come and see me work, you can fly up or drive over and come and see me work this coming Friday. But I'm going to charge $100."

Now, it was not because I needed $100 of course - but I wanted to attach q value to watching me work. It is a big deal. (I think it's a big deal!) I'm a top producer and I was willing to let someone watch me work for $100. It's worth much more, but the lesson is this: at some point you need to place a value on your time and experience. Because you are worth it!

One couple said, "We'll fly over and be there Friday morning," before anyone else had a chance. "Fine," I said, "Friday is just a normal work day for me, but remember, when you are here don't expect me to be your host or to take care of you. I'm going to be busy. Bring your lunch because your job is to just watch, make notes, and listen and observe."

Friday arrived.

The couple showed up, Nancy and Richard. Now Richard was a bit passive, and had a bit of an 'I'm more important than you are because I used to be an engineer attitude', but Nancy was the brains, was very sincere, and the real worker of the two.

They pulled out $200 and sat down. Richard spent a lot of time on his laptop. But Nancy paid close attention to everything.

Now I had bunch of leads from my postcard campaign - I had taken the messages off my 800 number voice mail, and was ready to start calling people back and make some quality conversations.

Nancy listened in on one of the telephone extensions so she could hear everything.

Well of course it would be today that Murphy's Law was the law of the land. The hours were going by fast, but I was getting nowhere.

Call after call was 'no one home', or 'not interested', or 'oh, who are you?' I was getting frustrated and I'm sure they were thinking "I'm not sure about Williams because what he's doing is nothing special and nobody is interested anyway."

I'll admit I was frustrated. I wanted to make something out of today - for myself – not because people were watching, (well, maybe just a bit!).

Now, this was my Mindset: to not go to bed without at least ONE positive call. Now there are days where my goal of 10 quality conversations doesn't get met. But never zero!

I said, "Look, I'm going to make at least one quality conversation today and that's that." It was already past 10:00 p.m., so I chose some numbers from Washington State where it was 3 hours earlier. I told Nancy and Richard, 'If you want to go back to the hotel, that's fine. If you want to stay and listen, that's fine too."

"It's okay, we'll stay," said Nancy, before Richard could even open his mouth.

Now here's where life becomes fun.

The LOA eventually paid off. LOA – The Law of Averages – (Not the Law of Attraction). The networker's best friend.

I had to call 3 numbers in Washington to get one live person. It turned out that he received my postcard, and had listened to my 5 minute voicemail message. Not only that but he remembered the postcard.

I asked him, "On a scale of 1 to 10, where are you?" Nancy fell out of her chair when she heard him say, "Eleven."

Richard was forced to sit down and take his coat back off.

This fellow - Randy –I'll never forget him – joined and made a minimum purchase right there and then over the phone and Internet. No webinar or anything. It was the postcards that did it - he said, 'I've been in networking for a long time but it was always the same - I never had anyone new to talk to, except the folks that were in the last program I was in. Your postcard was magic. Right away I wanted to know how you did it."

Now this was long before I did postcard training for anyone except members of my team – and I certainly did not have my book out. But Randy's joining made me feel better than when someone joined and placed a big product order. Just because I had been having such a bad day.

My Attitude that morning had started high, went low, lower to really low, and then ended high.

Yet my actions did not change: Following up my postcard leads by making my calls.

That's because, while my attitude went low, my Mindset did not change.

It's all about Doing – not how you feel.

NOTE: If you want one more success clue, it's about making that one extra call, taking that one extra step, or going the extra mile.

The bottom line is this: it's the Doing – the action is more important than our feelings or our Attitude.

My Attitude went up and down, but I just kept going. I didn't doubt my product or my business or myself or my postcard. I just kept going and trusted my actions.

By the way – Nancy ended up happily married to someone else and is now very high up in another program. We still keep in touch.

I don't know what Richard is doing.

The magic of the DMO

Once you start tracking your numbers - and I mean daily - you'll find that you want to beat your record, or at least your numbers from the day before.

This was my main reason for making that extra call. I did not want to have one day without at least one good quality conversation.

That day just ended up with one quality conversation – and it happened to be a 'yes'. I felt rewarded when I wrote about that victory in my business journal!

That brings me to the magic.

When you track yourself, you do more.

And you know what?

You take that extra step to squeeze out one more call…

It's usually that extra step, that extra mile, or in this case it was that extra call that made the difference.

You don't know who they know or what they are prepared to do. I did not know that this guy was just waiting for a system like the postcards so he could start networking again.

He turned out to be a great leg, and he built a huge retail customer base too. You just never know.

And because you don't know, don't judge that extra call. Just do it and do the best that you can to beat your own record.

Beware of Saboteurs!

If I don't get my daily behavior right, I'll never get my business right. If you don't get your daily behavior right, you will never get your business right.

When we don't get our daily behavior right it's because of self-sabotage.

Self-sabotage is the reason that good people are not successful in our industry. They join us and have seemed to have been successful in other endeavors, but fall victim to self-sabotage.

Make no mistake, when we are not performing our DMO, it's all because of self-sabotage.

It's true for all areas of our lives – but I'm not going to go into any other area – we'll just stick to our business.

Ask yourself:

"What's preventing me from picking up the phone?"

Guess what? In our business you never know who you are going to sponsor. That one person could go on to create a leg that earns you $1000's of dollars.

Each person I would enroll would motivate me.

I would think of the potential of that person.

Who did they know?

What cold market would they tap into?

How many postcards could they blast out and effectively follow up on?

It's exciting!

So what about YOU?

What keeps getting in your way that prevents you from Doing? From taking productive action continuously? Why do people take time off? Why do they turn the TV on and stop to make a personal call during production hours and then chit chat for an hour or two?

If you were working in an office, you wouldn't be able to do that. It's prohibited behavior.

Yet we do it.

That's what we call a 'stuck-block'.

A stuck-block is an activity that has a high 'stickiness factor'.

Like watching TV, surfing the web, answering email, Facebook, Pinterest, online trading accounts, etc., etc.

Full Disclosure: One of my stuck-blocks was online news. I just had to see what was up. I actually look back and feel 'disgusted' with the loss of productive time.

Why is it that people get stuck? We know when we do these things that it's not in accordance with our strict goal or our DMO or our personal contract. We know because there's a little feeling in the pit of our stomach telling us it's not right. Guilt.

We are guilty of self-sabotage.

It's a personal behavior.

It's personal behavior that has to change.

So how do we change that behavior?

Simple: You identify that behavior or highlight that behavior and then you delete it.

You delete that behavior by replacing it with something else.

You replace it with proper behavior from your strict DMO.

Remember this is a business. Just like McDonald's is a business.

They only have one method of operation that's effective. They don't let anyone experiment or make changes.

Never going to happen.

The Golden Arches has a very strict DMO. That's why McDonald's has more money than some countries. They don't leave their success to chance.

Imagine you are an 18 year old and working in McDonald's. Your manager or shift supervisor enforces a strict DMO that works - and guess what? You follow it and you're effective. You also notice that many of your supervisors are younger than you!

I remember speaking to one of my team who worked part time as a manager at McDonalds. He kept getting calls on his phone while we were doing some training. Exasperated with the interruption I told him to just take the call to end the distraction.

It turned out there was a shift where the manager/owner was ill, and they wanted this 19 year old to run the entire restaurant for a few days. After he finished his call, he saw a text from his mom, complaining about his messy bedroom.

He was a disciplined kid, a role model to the other workers and chosen to run the whole operation when the 45-year-old owner was unable to. He was in charge of people older than himself and ran an efficient restaurant.

But his bedroom?

If you asked his mother about his discipline, work ethic, etc., she might give you a very different story.

Had she wanted him to really change, she should have stop nagging and provide him with a strict DMO.

I've been told by some parents, after hearing this training in person, that they assigned a DMO to their teen and found it worked! Now that's leadership!

The DMO is all part of the same business magic that makes systems so much a buzz-word in business today.

Reduce your business to a system, turn that system into a DMO for you or any employee, and your business can be done by anyone – good Attitude or not – teenager or senior citizen – it's all about the DMO.

It's not Attitude, it's the DO! Once you DO, the Attitude will follow.

Sadly, most MLM trainers focus on Attitude as the sole message of their motivational trainings.

I did too until I learned about the DMO and Mindset.

As Zig said, "A great motivation speech wears off, like the effects of a bath." You need to take them over and over and over again if you want to base your success on Attitude.

Ask yourself: Who is going to take the time to change you?

Your upline is not responsible for your actions. Your spouse is not, your parents are not, only you are responsible for your actions. Others will try and influence you, but they are NOT responsible and because they have their own agenda - their bottom line not yours – so you can't allow them to direct your time. For example ABC, CBS, BBC, iTunes, Netflix, video games, Pinterest, Facebook, the list is endless.

Your chosen daily agenda is your DMO. Follow it.

When you take stock of your life you may find that you don't like the house you live in, your neighborhood, the school your kids are going to, the clothes you are wearing or your vacations. Clearly you have to change something.

YOU have to change something so what will it be?

YOU change your DMO, your actions.

Once you change your action, you'll become more effective, and within time, you'll change too. You will find the tasks we do as networkers more fun, easier, and soon your bank account will change, and so will your neighborhood!

As Zig Zigler would say: do a checkup from the neck up and figure out what activities you need to change.

Identify, delete, and replace.

You just switch from a poor activity to a productive one.

You know it happens with others - you have seen people making rapid changes to their life. Suddenly they're effective and making a lot of money.

How?

They changed one activity for another.

That could be you very soon!

How? By making it more painful for you to NOT follow your DMO. It must become painful for you to NOT make notes and to DO. It must be painful to NOT track yourself and do your follow-up calls. If life is 'OKAY' like my lawyer's was, you won't make the effort.

If you are satisfied by 'OKAY' there is not much we can do.

As Jim Rohn says, "You must become 'disgusted' with OKAY."

Why make your aim 'OKAY'?

What kind of a goal is it achieve "OKAY"?

Tom Peters calls it the 'we're no worse than anyone else' plan.

Is that a worthy plan, to be NO WORSE than anyone else?

No.

Once you become disgusted by your situation you will ACT - if only to avoid the disgust!

But here's the bright side: Eventually you don't need to dwell on the pain/disgust as motivation to act– you just follow your DMO by habit!

So focus on the pain and follow your DMO - make your plan and just go for it because that's the right thing to do to achieve your goals. On the days you feeling 'not doing anything' revisit the pain of what 'not doing' will bring back.

The "Event" that is Mindset magic – if you figure it out

You are not alone.

Everybody can use some help.

Don't be a stranger to your upline. Talk to your sponsor and those who are paid on your performance or whose team you are in. If you don't feel your sponsor is positive or a worthy mentor, keep going upline till you find someone who is. A good upline is like a business coach.

Talk to sideline too.

But there is one more place that is mandatory for our Mindset: 'EVENTS'

Sure, there are a lot of benefits for Attitude that an event brings you. However, I personally believe events can benefit your Mindset far greater than Attitude – if you are proactive.

We all know that just being at an event will change our Attitude. You'll be on a high from being around all that success and motivation. You will have some of the best emotional experiences of your life at events.

When you fly or drive home, you will be totally excited and pumped.

So if you only change your Attitude by attending an event you will find that the effect wears off in a few days.

Why?

Because Attitude is like a hot bath, remember?

Because absorbing the excitement at a conference is passive, i.e., you don't have to do anything to get that excitement – and this is sadly the only benefit that most people come away with.

While there are trainings at these conferences, most of them are not too different from what you have been taught before. Most are just watered down versions of the same-old same-old.

But let me explain to you how to adjust your Mindset at events.

When you get to an event, you have a lot of breaks, you have a lot of lunches, you have lots of dinners, cocktail parties, etc.

Can a few minutes be valuable? Hey, ask anyone who's been treated by a chiropractor. In 5 minutes they can fix you.

Let me share a story with you.

I went to a big event sponsored by my company. It was packed.

I was talking to everybody that I didn't know. I think people wondered about me. I was talking to everyone. I was introducing myself to everyone, asking questions and making notes in my notebook. Some people looked at me strangely, "Who's this guy taking notes?" But I took this event very seriously – I could meet people from all over the world who were doing the same business as I was, yet were doing it in different ways. That's why I went to the event. To learn those different ways. The idea – for me – was to avoid network marketing 'inbreeding' where distributors only know what their upline knows or is willing to teach.

Networking Success Clue for Leaders: Never stop learning how other people generate leads. Adopt, Adapt, and Improve. (That doesn't mean you need to use them all!)

I went to enjoy the time with my team too, but also I went to the event to bring something home with me as far as building my business.

I was talking to everybody and making notes, and sometimes even recording our talks. I noticed a guy who looked very sloppy. But something told me to go up to him. I asked him if he was new, was this his first event?

"No, this is my 10th."

I offered him my card and I took his.

Hold on, I looked at his card and saw his name and title. He was at the top of our compensation plan. I had not heard of him, but that was not unusual. Yet he did not look the part of the typical 'success profile' image that you see going across the stage.

He really looked like a guy dressed to get on a greyhound bus or to walk into a bingo hall.

Now I was very curious. I asked him how he achieved his position.

"Hard work," he said.

I wanted to know more. I asked him how he found people. You see, that is what I ask everyone. And I never cared if people asking me how I did it either. Back then, I was doing some ads and other things that were not working too well.

At some point in time, he realized I wasn't going away.

He said, "Okay, I'll tell you what I do. I send letters in the mail, I do enough to get 2 to 3 people a week to our meetings. I do some mailings outside my city and have 2 or 3 people on our conference calls too. I know how many letters to send to get enough leads for me to work on each week. It's not a big deal."

By doing that, he and his team became a recruiting machine, but he liked to keep that to himself.

He would not get into details, but I did tell his story in my book *How to Prospect and Recruit using Postcards for a MLM or Network Marketing Business: The Low cost Prospecting and Recruiting Tool that Out Performs Online Methods*, so I'm not going to repeat it here. This is a book on Mindset, not recruiting methods.

Here was a guy who was at the top, but was not acting like a big shot, not at all. He was just a relaxed happy guy. But what he told me impacted me big time. He doesn't even know how much, but I knew the entire conference was nothing compared to me learning that one idea.

I walked from our coffee table dizzy. I said to myself, "I'm going to make a lot of money this year."

Just that coffee was worth all the money I paid to fly in and attend that conference. Just that short meeting made a major impact on my business, and allowed me to prospect using direct mail, letters, postcards, etc., all over the world without ever worrying about 'where to find people' etc. Talk about how powerful events are!

But the point of me relating this story to you is NOT the power of direct mail, (which is really powerful), but that you must attend events with the goal of learning tactics for your DMO.

The biggest mistake I see leaders make is promoting events to folks just so they come back 'pumped'.

Sure events are motivating, but do you want to know what motivation is?

What it really is?

I'll tell you, and few people can boil it down to once sentence, (even if I can't write the preamble in a few words):

Motivation is just realizing that 'you can'.

Right?

We attend one of those great motivating sessions by Tony Robbins, Brian Tracy, the late Jim Rohn, or even someone in your upline. When you come out of that room you believe you are 10 feet tall and bulletproof!

Me too! It happens to all of us.

We fly home, drive home, or float home – empowered by the event.

Because we understand, "I can."

But soon we are home.

The next day we face the same negative spouse or work-mates, the same old tired prospect list we had in our computer, the same bills and challenges that were there before we left.

And soon we lose the "I can Attitude" and it morphs into "I can't…I wish I could, but my situation is different, it's fine for everyone else, but not me…maybe I just need to find something else instead…"

Why?

Because nothing's changed.

Who cares that the company released a new product.

If you can't build a team with the old products, why would you think you can with the new one? _____ Note

So for me, motivation is like candy. I like it, but I don't want too much.

I look for substance.

I look for protein.

Protein lasts.

Protein is a metaphor for methods of generating leads – which means taking action.

Candy is a metaphor for Attitude.

For me, the best thing about the conference is coming back with additions or changes for my DMO.

New things to DO that will advance my prospecting. Could be a new recruiting video, or prospecting tool, a good 'line' or phrase that makes explaining what we sell or our comp plan easier to show our prospects.

Sometimes you hit gold like I did by being introduced to a new lead generating method.

I always want to know where people find prospects, what is their sales process, their success ratio, i.e., their numbers, what they say on the phone. When I get home all of these practical things that will be added to my DMO once I decide I want to use them.

I make note of the rest that I don't use too.

Sometimes I find that there are things that I don't want to do but might be really suited to someone in my team – and I teach that team member that tactic.

Once more I want to mention duplication. Look, you may have an upline who is a telemarketing type – a real pro on the phone. Or perhaps is someone who knows SEO and Internet Marketing. If you are attracted to that or are comfortable there, you duplicate. But not everyone is. So if you know a variety of methods to generate leads – besides 'buying Internet leads' – you will go far.

I know people ask, "But what is the BEST lead generation method?" There is no BEST method, you pick the best method for YOU to use at the time. If someone asks you what is the best method, overview all the different methods and ask them to choose. If they still don't know, they must experiment on their own to find out. Just caution them on spending a lot of money as they experiment. I don't work with people who can't make a decision. If you chose for them they will hold you accountable. Especially if they don't work!

You want to recruit those who know themselves well. Don't go over-board on duplication – it does not mean to blindly-copy your upline – you are responsible to find a lead generation method that works for YOU.

Bottom Line: Go to events and ask people specific questions – especially people you don't know or are from far away. Ask them what their upline does, or teaches, ask them what they say on the phone. Sure lots of it will be the same, that's OKAY. But eventually you'll learn a new method, idea or tactic that will make you more money and help your team.

How to ask people in your company – that you don't know – how they find leads – without feeling uncomfortable.

Is asking people you don't know how they work the business uncomfortable? Yes. Being uncomfortable is part of our business. If you are having trouble with opening a conversation with someone say this: "Hi, (intro yourself, from your-town), and I'd like to ask you a question – its making me a bit uncomfortable so pardon me – but I'd really like to hear someone else's view on this – what do you say on the phone to a prospect (this will give you script ideas – record this with permission), or, what have you found that works to generate leads?

Be prepared to make notes! Once you say you are uncomfortable people melt and want to help you. I still say now.

Does that mean every new idea you learn will work?

Does that mean every new idea you have will work?

No.

Let me take a second to tell you about just one of the MANY crazy things I tried.

Do you ever order pizza delivered to your home?

Of course you do.

So do I.

I figured if I order in pizza, so would other top potential networkers.

So I went to my local pizza joint. Now I was a single guy back then and had no cooking skills. This was something I overlooked when I had this idea. The classic marketing mistake of believing everyone is like you.

I went to speak to the owner of the parlor. I told him I wanted to put a large sticker on the inside of 1000 pizza boxes. He laughed and said 'why not' – for $300! It had headline like: Need a second income? (lame, I know)? Call me now. And to top it off, I put in my personal cell phone number.

Can you imagine how may calls I got night after night from pizza chomping wealth seekers?

None. No one called.

Not even a complaint about the pizza!

I even ordered a few pizzas to be sure the stickers were inside the box covers!

Later I read the demographics.

Most folks who ordered pizza are NOT your ideal prospects.

Ask yourself who orders a lot of pizza?

It seems it's not a group that cares about making a second income – not many 'wealth-builders' have Domino's on speed-dial. Mostly it's those eating pizza from the box, watching TV all night and playing video games, (and smoking an herb which is now legal in Colorado!)

Okay, so it was a dumb idea.

That's why it's not the subject of a book, it's just an example of all the things I tried, tested and DID.

Every time I think of this crazy idea, it reminds me of an old Frank Sinatra song. One of the lines in the song is: *Do you remember the men who had to fall to rise again. Take a deep breath, dust yourself off and start over again.*

What if you are not succeeding with your current DMO?

How can you fix it?

First, trust in yourself. Trust in your decisions. As we previously discussed, trust in yourself to pick the right method of prospecting once you have a fair idea of a few different approaches, (which will determine your DMO).

Second, meditation.

Yes, meditation.

What's meditation?

Meditation is essentially slowing down your brain frequency.

We need to slow down our brain frequency because our brain frequency is pretty fast.

We need to slow our brains down to be able to tap into what we have learned (like tactics for our DMO) and to think about these things. Then we can analyze them. We slow down our thinking.

For example, we visualize ourselves delivering telephone or direct conversations very confidently. Recruiting new people that are good and we visualize their success. If you learn a new idea, visualize all the steps you need to do to get it going. Once I learned about direct mail, I went home and bought books and became an expert on it. Don't expect someone to teach you HOW to do it, you just need to know WHAT to do and you can learn the rest by visualizing the steps you need to take to put your method together, or to follow it.

Make a note of these steps, they will become your DMO.

Once I read all the books I could on direct mail, I visualized how I would apply it to our industry. Eventually I found that mailing 10 postcards per day perfect and it became a permanent part of my DMO.

If you need help with ideas, Google is your friend! So is Amazon – buy books and study.

This is why we need to 'slow down to speed up'.

You make your plans when you slow down your brain – that is the best way to influence your subconscious. If you need some additional aids for that, look in the resources section and I'll share with you something that really improved not only me but everyone on my team that used them.   You will find the only Hypnosis CD's I recommend.

What *about* YOU?

I'll bet you have more going for you than you think you have.

Do this exercise and find out.

We're going to take inventory.

Write down these 3 letters vertically on the page where you have been taking notes. You have been taking notes, right?

Write BAG, but like this:

B
A
G

Yes, BAG.

We are going to take inventory to create 'confidence builders'. This will help us take action with confidence.

First is B.

Be thankful for your blessings. You are blessed with certain things, certain gifts. You're blessed with your Attitudes, with your behavior, perhaps with good looks, with your emotions, with your family, with your friends, intelligence. We're all blessed with many things different from each other.   Perhaps you are a confident person already. Just as we must play the hand we've been dealt, we also have positive advantages, or blessings.

Don't use my examples as a guide, you MUST list your own blessings. If you are thinking right now that you don't have any – please do yourself a favor and quit MLM. It is not for you, and that is the best advice I can give you. Because there is no one reading this that is not blessed with something.

A is for accomplishments. What have you accomplished in the past? Write them down. Do it, take the time now and do this.

We all have a lot of accomplishments starting from early childhood. Many of these we forget or take for granted. Perhaps you have a university degree – which you think is worthless. It's not. It's valuable in so many ways. Even if you never 'use' it.

In your hobbies, maybe you excelled in Girl Guides, or Scouts long ago. Write it down. I can tell you that you that you have accomplished something with flying colors in your past. Go back and dwell on those thoughts and add them to your list.

Some of my best team leaders told me they had accomplished little. "What about your kids?" I ask.

"Oh, well if you count them…I'm a big winner!"

Of course we count them. If you have raised your kids successfully, you have accomplished so much that counts towards your networking success. There's much more that I could say about the hardest working people I know – woman networks. Many are Mom's too!

If I paid you $1000 for each accomplishment that you list, I'll bet I'd owe you plenty!

We each have a lot of accomplishments, which means that we are going to have to continue our accomplishment trend!

In other words you will accomplish your goals. Depend on it!

G is gratification.

What gives you gratification? People, places, things, travel, your family, your business, learning, walking across the state? Moving outside your comfort zone and being all the bigger for it?

One thing that gives us gratification is success. What were your past successes? What are your future successes? Write them down now.

You see gratification is important. Especially as networkers. We are in a business where there is a lot of rejection. That is why there is big money to be earned. It's the only reason there is so much money. If there were no rejection, there would be no money. So embrace it by knowing what gives you gratification.

Make that list and reward yourself from that list what it's appropriate. For myself I would work all out for 90 days and take a week vacation. A beach was on my list of gratification. It's different for each of us.

The fact is each of us talks to people on a daily basis and most don't buy what we've got. They don't buy our ideas. They don't buy our products. They don't join our business.

And on the subject of rejection...

Let's make one thing clear: You can't be responsible for other people's behavior - what they do or don't do. What they say or don't say. You cannot be responsible. You're only responsible for your own behavior. You can't change anyone but yourself.

I remember waiting to speak at a conference where Les Brown was the main attraction.

The guy is amazing. If you ever have a chance to hear him, take it. Les has power.

Anyway, during the Q & A, a fellow in the back asked, "How do I change my prospect? How do I change them to want to join my company?"

Les said, "I've been trying to change my twin brother for the last 50 years. I decided I made a big mistake and wasted a lot of time with that effort. I was never able to change him. I just couldn't. I've been successful and I wanted him to be too, but I just couldn't change him."

That's Les Brown, one of the best influencers in the world.

A powerful lesson for each of us to never forget.

What can you do to change somebody? You can't. You do your best possible job to assist someone who wants to change themselves and then you move on. Remember they are as responsible for their life as you are for yours.

You're not responsible for them.

As a double check, just ask whose taking responsibility for your life before taking on anyone else's.

No one. Just you. And you're GREAT!

Putting it all together

We must depend on Mindset – not attitude – to carry out our DMO

This is why we must alter ourselves.

We can only do this by changing our behavior, not by a 'nice hot motivational bath'.

We change our behavior through our DMO and sticking to it.

We do it by making a DMO that leads us to our long-term strategic goal.

By following our DMO we overcome the negative that is there.

This is our Mindset. To DO, to ACT on the Daily Method of our Operation.

Our Mindset is set to command our body to act.

Not to change how we feel, just to act.

We pick up the phone and we don't allow negative prospects to get under our skin. We do this by simply moving on and making the next call – by DOING.

When we set up a little meeting or a house presentation we acknowledge we may be nervous be we just go and DO.

When you keep on moving (acting or doing), negativity won't have time to creep in.

You need to move on. If a prospect is not interested that's just fine. "Thank you for sharing, Ms. Prospect, goodbye. Have a nice day."

(But never forget to say: "Hey, can I drop you a line by email every once in a while to keep in touch?" Because you never know what changes in their life down the road will cause them to email you back – hence my email campaign – see the Resources section.)

When prospects say 'no' it's their problem. It's not your problem, just move on.

Think about it:

Ask yourself, "What is the worst possible situation that can happen in this business? Somebody says no, that's it! What's the worst case scenario?"

Ask yourself another question after you hang up the phone from a 'no': Are you still alive? Are you still okay? Have you survived? Of course!

You still have the ability to start over by picking up the phone and calling the next person by following your DMO.

The 4 Steps to Mindset Success

What are you doing to sabotage yourself?

Whatever it is, just turn it off. Whatever it is, turn it off so it cannot sabotage you anymore. What's getting in your way? What do you need to change? How much money is it costing you? How much time are you losing from your family by 'playing networker'?

How much money has your bad behavior cost you?

Bad behavior like not making follow up calls? Not generating leads or finding a lead system that works for you?

Not keeping your success posture?

Not attending events, trainings, or reading books like this one?

Not tracking your actions?

Not having a personal contract with yourself?

Not keeping a journal?

Being slow in getting back to people, talking too much, apologizing too much?

How much is it costing you in real numbers?

Remember the secret that we covered already:

It's NOT how you feel that will determine how you act. Its how you act that determines how you feel.

For example, you signed up a new person – ask yourself 'How do you feel?"

Aren't you feeling great?

Of course.

The secret of success is knowing what to DO - AND doing it. Both.

But only you can DO.

We can teach you what to do but only you can take action. Forget waiting for a 'positive mental Attitude'. Just Do and your PMA will come up shyly behind you and try and take all the credit for your Mindset's success!

What to DO is just a set of skills, or a skillset. Knowing what to DO and getting good at it is a matter of knowing and doing over and over and over again.

You pay attention to your actions, you record them in your journal, and you practice by Doing. The result will be that you get better and better faster and faster.

That's the great thing about this business. You can practice on real people. All those people who say 'no' are helping you. If you quit after 50 'no's', you wasted a lot of learning.

You're practicing. Say thank you to those folks who said 'no'. Be grateful you have sparring partners for free. That's what creates your skillset.

They will keep giving you feedback – and that feedback will teach you how to act.

Because you now know 'how you act determines how you feel', you can manage your Mindset to always be productive and effective.

Repletion through action creates success.

Follow the steps:

1) Determine your lead, prospecting and follow up process or system. Record the process or steps, based on that go to step 2

2) Create your DMO – write it out – put it where you can see it in your home-office as you work

3) Make a contract with yourself to carry out your DMO – strictly!

Are you willing to do something about your life and business to make a contract with yourself? Are you committed to doing whatever it takes? The real winners make it happen.

They don't wait for it to happen. They make it happen. This is not a 'saying', this is a rule.

4) You must ACT on your DMO on a daily basis.

You must increase your actions to get better and better at whatever you are not doing well. You must put in the numbers and practice. As you get better so does your Attitude!

Winners believe in their decision and they push themselves to get better and better with their skillset. And, they never stop doing it.

The winner does not trust in only their Attitude – they trust in knowing what to do (DMO) and Action, (following the DMO).

We were all there once. I was there. I know how you feel. I know what you're going through and I KNOW you will take action.

Email me and tell me what you have gained from this book and how I can serve you better.

I care about each of you.

David Williams

DavidWilliamsMLMAuthor@gmail.com

Resources

Audios:

The Fastest way to Networking Perfection: **Rapid Business Hypnosis CD's and MP3 downloads**. These are the ONLY Hypnosis CD's I recommend and use.

From my Desk:

Want to know the $9.99 tool that increased my production massively in one month? Sorry, but you can't buy it from me.

Now this tool has been out for just 3 years, but only a few clever networkers are sharing it with their team. However I have seen the results first hand – on myself – and my team – and I believe anyone in our industry who has not achieved their goals NEED's to use this simple, inexpensive and very effective 'unfair advantage'.

I remember just how I discovered these. It was a few years ago and I was frustrated with some negative attitudes that were showing themselves just after the 2008 crash. It was all over the TV, social media, the radio, every place you went. Times got tough and you could feel it.

I knew that no matter how strong our Mindset was, the negativity was going to attack us. And just like any army that is strong enough to withstand an attack it can still hurt!

I had an opportunity to do some consulting with a fellow who was an expert in the mind, and how to influence it by hypnosis and other techniques. I was approached to consult with the company that he chose to produce his CDs and audio downloads. They needed someone to write some advertising copy about his products for their sales page. I did not have time to take the contract, but I was totally convinced by all the science I saw.

They had titles that were about Abundance, Creating Wealth, Law of Attraction, etc. Even some about general sales. They offered me a few to try, but since I turned down their job offer, I felt better by paying for them.

I started with the Abundance and Wealth Creation hypnosis MP3s and after one week, I could 'notice' a difference.

The benefits really showed after the 4th week of use. Profound is not the word for it. I found that my production was up, and that meant more and more money. I could see the results in my bottom line - where results count!

I was also 'attracting' far better prospects, and I eliminated poor prospects faster. It was amazing. For me this was just so fantastic!

I did two things:

First I MADE (not asked) all of my team leaders to purchase their own copy, and use them.

Sure I could have copied mine – but I have learned from experience – things given for free are not used. Value must be felt by the user – and the best way to have them feel the value is for them to pay too. Don't forget this lesson.

Second I told the people behind these amazing hypnosis audios that they need to create some for the network marketing industry, and not just 'generalized' but very specific. I told them they need to deal with follow-up, 'the heavy phone syndrome', feeling negative about sales, seeking good prospects, Law of Attraction, etc. I gave them a big list!

They took my advice and set them up for sale online about 3 years ago for $39.99 for each album.

But NO! They are NOT $39.99!

I implored them to offer them on Apple and Amazon so all networkers could find them. Today all of these powerful and life changing audios can be found on iTunes, Amazon MP3, Google Play, Beats Music, Spotify, Rhapsody, Emusic, & MediaNet for $9.99!

If you are in a rush, just search for "Rapid Hypnosis Success Network Marketing MP3" on Amazon or iTunes, Google Play etc. Get all 5 albums, or you can buy a few MP3s from each set for .89 cents each.

These MP3's are on the iPads, iPods and other devices of not only me, but the key members of all of my teams. And while I am not 'active' anymore, I listen to at least one of them weekly.

I decided it was high-time to share this secret advantage with everyone.

Sadly, I know many 'top dogs' who use these too, yet don't want anyone else to known about them. They are trapped in the 'old school' competition trap.

Ok, take a look at what you get on the first album Network Marketing Rapid Mindset Hypnosis Success - Volume 1 (There are 40 tracks on each album):

- I Love Prospecting - Hypnotic Suggestions for Network Marketing Day 1
- Become Persistent & Consistent - Hypnotic Suggestions for Network Marketing Day 1
- Eliminating the Fear of No's - Hypnotic Suggestions for Network Marketing Day 1
- Winning Network Attitude - Hypnotic Suggestions for Network Marketing Day 1

Just go to your favorite online music story and search:

"Rapid Hypnosis Success Network Marketing"

Find and order all 5.

There are no affiliate links here – I'm giving this info to you because I have really seen the positive change in – not only myself – but in entire teams, large groups, and at least one company who ordered them for each distributor.

So today, do your business a favor, invest in yourself and get a hold of this unfair advantage right now!

Books:

How to Recruit Doctors into your MLM or Network Marketing team by showing them a NO Warm Market System

- Where to Find Doctors – It's not where you think
- A new source of Doctors (medical) who are not busy
- Perfect for the Wellness Industry
- No buying Leads
- Not working the phone

This book is going to teach you an amazing system to recruit Doctors and an amazing system for you to build a huge, profitable and unstoppable leg under them - without the Doctor using any of their warm market, 'buying leads' or touching the phone!

Full Discloser: This is a short book. It's less than 50 pages long. It contains no fluff or padding. It's direct and to the point. The system contained is worth hundreds of thousands of dollars in sales, and could retire you. Really. Forget the low price of $8.99, forget the number of pages. This book will show you a fool proof system that ANY one can follow to build an unstoppable MLM Network Marketing business by recruiting Doctors. I have made it newbie friendly, but those with experience will take this system and put into practice very quickly.

This book will cover, step by step, and in very detailed and specific language:

The 'invisible' secret source of Doctors without a practice that are begging for something like what you will be able to show them

How to recruit busy Doctors with a practice and zero time

How to avoid the 'I don't want to go to my contacts/warm market' objection because you will be teaching them a system that requires ZERO warm market

And No 'buying leads'!

How to fill, yes FILL, meeting rooms with prospects all eager to join and try your products

NO conference calls, webinars, websites, Fanpages, autoresponders etc.

This is the full system, from the free ads you will place to the words on the marketing material you will print. This approached is very inexpensive to follow, quick and easy to implement, and very straight forward.

Also included are the phone scripts and person to person scripts you need to use when speaking to the Doctors, their receptionists, and to use in getting the appointment.

Forget all the 'usual suspects' techniques, this is not about dropping off DVDs, inviting them to conference calls, or creating special 'Doctors only' presentations. Forget all of that, and forget all of your old scripts and ads.

This system works for Doctors and requires NO Warm Market – I know I said that above, but it's very important you know this. You don't need any paid advertising, Facebook, Internet, Twitter etc., this is all offline, local, and affordable. No one has taught you this before. Guaranteed.

MLM Script Treasury: Not Your Usual Network Marketing Phone Scripts

This book is full of the top pulling, most valuable and very rare MLM phone scripts that have earned their users many hundreds of thousands of dollars. I will say right now, the material in this book is NOT 'newbie' friendly. These scripts are for pros. If you don't know what you're doing this book is not for you.

- Turn your prospects voice mail into a recruiting machine! 12 scripts which you can customize
- What do I say to make sure my prospects watch's my DVD or online presentation?
- What is a GAP line and why you should use one, and what to say on it.
- How to take your prospects pulse
- Top Tier Phone scripts – rare and valuable – and great to modify for your own phone scripts
- What to say to get your prospect on to a conference call
- How to close your prospect after a conference call – lots of trial closes, hard closes, and objection handlers
- Common objections and how to turn them back into closing questions

I have chosen scripts that I know you will NOT find in other script books for sale, or the free PDFs that float all over the Internet. The scripts contained here are the kind of scripts that only the top leaders in a program have access to and it usually requires someone to be invited to join their inner team to gain access to them.

- Scripts to get a prospect to commit to a live conference call
- The hardest closing questions from the industry
- Ads that will get your Voice Mail full, and what to say on your Voice Mail screener – lots of screeners and out bound messages
- What to say to your prospect AFTER the conference call
- Voice Scripts to 'wake up the dead' – get your inactive distributors active again
- Starting your own MLM or Team Call? Need a conference call script? – 4 full conference call scripts inside
- Are you a company trainer? Do you do many trainings? Are your people dying on the phone?

If you are a trainer, a serious upline, on your way to being a player, a 'big dog', this book is for you. If you are putting together your own scripts, calls, establishing your own team, or your own network marketing company – invest in this book. Inside this book you will find: hard hitting, hard closing power calls, what to say when you reach a prospects voice mail, screeners, actual company conference calls, GAP line messages and some special bonuses to get your phone ringing plus much, much more. It's all here.

What is in this book can take a serious player to the next level.

This is most definitely an 'insider's book'.

MLM Autoresponder Messages and Network Marketing Email Messages: Financial Woes Pack

This book contains a professionally written email drip campaign of 30 powerful, engaging and entertaining persuasive email/autoresponder messages focused on your prospects 'Financial Woes' and how YOU can help your prospect solve them.

Warning!

If you have been in Network Marketing for any length of time, you probably have accumulated a list of prospects and their email address. However, many of these prospects have entered the 'witness protection program'. In other words, they never call back or reply to your emails. Most people forget about this list, but there is GOLD in it!

Now, you probably have an email system you pay for that is filled with 'canned' autoresponders about your company, or even some generic versions to send to your list. Some-times this is part of your 'back-office'.

But, have you read these autoresponders being sent in your name?

They're terrible!

Here's why:

You have a prospect who is looking to solve THEIR problem, which is lack of money. They need money, income, some light at the end of the tunnel, cash, maybe some dough to save their home... BUT they are NOT shopping for a MLM company, an INDUSTRY, or how long your company has been in business, or even what your product does...NO... they are desperate for a SOLUTION to their problems!

But if all the emails you send out are about 'the company, the timing, the industry...or how someone else is making money' – no wonder they don't bother responding to you!

Your prospect doesn't care about other people's wealth when THEY are broke and in financial pain. In fact, it works the other why. Resentment, suspicion, distrust.

Their mind is on their lack of money and they are worried.

They are awake all night worrying about their debt because they are in financial trouble.

And what? You send them an email about how old your company is?

It's basic marketing; offer your prospect a solution to their problem, and relate to them on their terms.

So, what is in this book? Do I teach you how to write emails? NO…NO…and NO!!!!

Is this some lessons on basic copy writing for MLM? Heck NO!!!

But let's face it. Most people can't write a note to save their lives, let alone a well-crafted email campaign. Forget learning a skill that will take you years to master – just use expert messages instead!

That's where this book of powerful 'financial woes' autoresponder messages will come to your aid.

Inside are 30 rock solid emails that focus on your prospects financial situation - with engaging humor and playfulness - showing how YOU and your program can help him out of his or her financial mess.

FULL DISCLOSURE – this is a small book – 30 powerful emails. You are not paying for the quantity of words, you are paying for the quality of the message and for getting your phone to ring.

This book contains 30 well-crafted powerfully written emails that and fun and engaging that will suggest and reinforce to your prospect that YOU are the answer to their financial problems using proven psychological and persuasion techniques.

Take these email autoresponder messages and enter them into your back-office or your email program. Start dripping on your list with these professionally written email messages – each crafted to have your prospect motivated to reach out and call YOU as an answer to their Financial Woes!

MLM Autoresponder Network Marketing Email Messages: Wellness Nutritional Pack

This is a completely different set of email messages then those in the above book. You can add these to the 30 in the above book, or use them on their own. However they are written just for networkers in wellness programs.

From the Description:

This book contains a professionally written email drip campaign of 30 powerful, engaging and entertaining persuasive email/autoresponder messages focused on the wellness industry.

If your products include wellness, nutritional or related products, this drip list campaign will engage your prospect and have them calling you. These autoresponder messages contain humor, personality, and are wellness/health/nutritional related.

They are perfect for the person who appreciates wellness or nutrition as a cause AND a vehicle for profit. It assumes that your prospect likes to 'help' people and has an interest in seeing the level of health improved.

Deregulation and Energy MLM Email Prospecting Autoresponder Messages: for Network Marketing companies offering Electricity or Natural Gas

This book contains a professionally written email drip campaign of 30 powerful, engaging and entertaining persuasive email/autoresponder messages focusing on the Energy industry.

These emails are perfect for North American Power, 5Linx, Veridian, CCM Consumer Choice Marketing, Momentis, IGNITE, Ambit, ACN - and any other energy or electricity network marketing company.

If your products include electricity, natural gas or related products, this drip list campaign will engage your prospect and have them calling you.

These autoresponder messages contain humor, personality, and are energy and deregulation related. They are perfect for the person who looking for a REAL residual income.

Each email ends with asking the prospect to call you now as the call to action.

How to Prospect and Recruit using Postcards for your MLM or Network Marketing Business The Low cost Prospecting and Recruiting Tool that Out Performs Online Methods

Fed up not having quality leads?

Are you in a MLM company you love, but just can't find REAL prospects to talk to?

Tried 'online' leads but found you just wasted your time and money?

Many networkers are well past the 'warm market' stage, and are struggling to find success. It seems the entire world has gone online and the problem that networkers face is sticking out in an ever increasing ocean of websites, mobile apps, opt-in forms, blog posts, Face-book Likes, YouTube movies and Tweets. It never ends.

There is alternative. There is another way.

Because the world HAS gone online, good old fashioned Direct Mail is making a come-back. Why? Because no one gets 'real' mail anymore. You have zero competition!

And what's more real than a picture postcard?

NOTE:

What This Book is NOT about: this book in no way teaches you to send those ugly, tacky, pre-printed, glossy pictures of fast expensive cars or mansions, or YELLOW 'print your own' postcards. NO, NO, NO!

If you are engaged in postcard marketing, buying glossy tacky 'in your face' MLM style postcards and mailing them out – or worse – paying to have them mailed out – I'll show you a method that will increase your success by a massive amount – because I guarantee your message will be read if you use the method I teach.

Or, if you are prospecting with one of those 'print your own' cards at the local Office Max, mailing out thousands until you're broke by sending ugly cards – you will be so happy switching to my method because it will save you time, money, you'll mail out less cards and get massive more results.

Again, because I guarantee your prospect will read your message.

I will show you a method that combines two of the most important recruiting factors for success in MLM:

Mass Recruiting and Personalization

And NO – this is not about using computer 'hand writing fonts'!!!

I'll show you a method to recruit massively with postcards, in a very personalized way for your prospect to find it impossible to not read your message and make a call.

This works.   This book is based on my famous Direct Mail for Networkers seminars that were part of a $10,000 MLM insider's weekend training. You will get this same information for less than $10. And the best part of it is, this system works even better today than before! Why? Because the power of a postcard, personalized, is stronger today in this Internet age.

Full Disclosure: This is a short, to the point book. It's not full of padding or fluff, (however, I do trace for you how I discovered my introduction into Direct Mail for MLM Recruiting by a presidential fundraiser).

It's a 'How To' book. You are paying for the system, the magic, and the fact that you won't need any other information to get started.

I have included low or no budget methods as well.

Please NOTE: This book is for MLM or Network Marketing recruiting – it's not about post-card 'marketing' for non-MLM business. The information here is for network marketers who want to build downlines and offer a system to their team that does not rely on 'buying leads' from the internet and telemarketing 'survey leads', 'real time leads', 'fresh leads', or any of the other scammy descriptions of absolutely terrible leads for sale by lead companies.

This system works in USA, Canada and Europe – I know because I have used it in each of those countries and built huge downlines in this way.

MLM and Network Marketing professionals guide to Recruiting Wellness: and Holistic Practitioners for 2014 The Wellness Industry Handbook for Exploding your Downline

By David Williams and Max Hailey

This book was written for you because you need to learn how to take advantage of 2014/15 - two years where there will be a MAJOR jump forward in the Wellness MLM industry.

Miss these steps and you will regret it. Check out just some of the Table of Contents:

1. Who and How to Recruit How to Brand yourself on the net Holistic Wellness:
2. The new Holy Grail Recruiting ground - if you do it right How to turn this 'Holistic' trend into a downline exploding movement
3. Wellness: The answer to the Health Crisis and an Engine for Income behind Network
4. Marketing Sharing of Wellness: Why Network Marketing The REAL reasons why Wellness has Become More Profitable for the Networker
5. How to create a Product Zealot
6. How to use the Increase of Baby Boomers and Active Older Adults to light a fire in your recruiting
7. Where to find Boomers Targeting the Fitness and Weight Loss Market 9 Reasons
8. Why Obesity will fatten your bank account
9. Why Leading with the Product is Insanely Bad advice
10. The 2 Words That Will Make Wealth for the Network Marketer
11. The 9 Key Wellness categories - Where is the money for Networkers

And much more...

The Simplest, Shortest, Most Powerful MLM and Network Marketing Prospect Control and Closing Lines and Scripts

Do you have trouble closing prospects? Do you feel you lose control of your prospecting and follow up calls? Do you have trouble closing strong prospects – the very ones you desperately want on your team?

Well, this book is for you. It's the lowest price but highest value book on Amazon. Why? Because this little book contains over 120 of the strongest, easiest, subtlest closing and 'keeping control' and 'taking control' over the conversation lines for network marketers.

FULL DISCLOSURE: This is a short book. This book has over 150 'lines'; mostly one line sentences. But don't be fooled by the size of the book. These are powerful closing lines to allow you to close your prospect. This is NOT a book on prospecting, recruiting or even a script book.

This is a book that should be open at your desk as you make your prospecting and follow up calls. If you find you prospect off their script (they never stay on script – only you can do that), these lines will bring you back into control.

They are subtle, but powerful. Here's some samples:

- How much does it cost?
- Millions of dollars not to get involved
- Can you see yourself taking people through a process just like I did with you?
- You can't outsource your learning
- The table's set
- This is thick
- I'm not claiming we have an automatic system, I'm demonstrating it
- Get into the game with us
- Let me layout how the business will start for you
- This is just a process to see if there a fit for you
- This is not a pressure gig
- It's just the way we do this (process)
- There's no glory in paying bills
- I promise I'm not going to push you, chase you or sell you

- I'm not going to come back to close you, but to personalize the business for you

Important message for Team Leaders:

If you would like any set of my emails personalized for your team or company, just contact me. I have a relationship with a company that will set you up. Just shoot me an email requesting more info and we can chat. This is the best way to take your team to the next level. I wish I had this kind of tool when I was active.

DavidWilliamsMLMAuthor@gmail.com

About the Author

If you want to know one thing about David Williams it's this:

He believes in OFFLINE prospecting and ONLINE follow up!

David Williams has been a top earner and top performer in networking for over 25 years. He has worked all over the world building teams successfully. In the last five years he has worked with corporations to develop MLM opportunities as well as top performers to create recruiting systems for their teams.

He also delivers 'insider only' high priced seminars for 'the big dogs' on practical MLM: prospecting, recruiting and team expansion.

Prior to Networking Williams' background was a few years of university – which meant he was broke.

In 2012 he decided to put into book-form some of the trainings he has done and offer them to anyone. Typically his work spreads word-of-mouth and word-of-mouse. Williams decided to present his insiders training at price levels that are affordable via the Internet to anyone but is not trying to disrupt the high priced seminars business either. Rather he feels that his readers are new and future leaders who are not even aware of these insider events but will one day will be seated there if they follow his systems.

Williams is not actively working any MLM program but enjoys 8 different residual income sources and in multiple currencies.

His favorite MLM tips include:

- Fire your Upline
- Be the Upline you want
- Never stop recruiting
- How much money would I make today if my downline did what I did?
- He hates 'fluff' training

He writes a MLM email training letter that he sends weekly - you can sign up too at www.DavidWilliamsMLMAuthor.com

Those who have signed up for David's newsletter may reach him via that email address. Feel free to contact him with any question.

Made in the USA
San Bernardino, CA
07 December 2015